the flap pamphlet series

The Sideways For It

open, read, turn

The Sideways For It

the flap pamphlet series (No. 16)
Printed and Bound in the United Kingdom

Published by the flap series, 2017
the pamphlet series of flipped eye publishing
All Rights Reserved

Cover Design by Petraski
Series Design © flipped eye publishing, 2010
Author Photo © Hazera Forth, 2017

ISBN-13: 978-1-905233-51-9

Contents | *The Sideways For It*

The Sideways For It

Ian McEwen

So what?

Those days he still
held the gold bell straight,   this is it -
sucking the liquorice   spirals
from the microphone   when the horn cuts in,   like a curl of smoke   unscripted
dynamic fluid   in the shape of light,   the only law   he claims
pours up,   frees itself,   is just
the ground   to stand
and take
the air.

Covent Garden in three acts

Her mirror winks: pretty mother watching the street act,
a juggler, but her lipstick is right now, she starts to drag
the toddler away. He, staring moon-faced, wants to stay
    she says 'Its just a trick. We've got to go – now!'
she belts the boy into the pushchair, scissors off

can't wait for the miracle from the man in motley,
but the entertainer is in the swing, flapping round
past the crowd. The child wails, but the juggler
    he goes the other way making klaxon cries,
and Doppler shifts, he's done it all before,

has learned to please his audience
    so natural in his practised tricks,
I'm old enough to know how this ends
    but stay to watch him run through the patter
and juggles he does all the time for his mirror.

If repetition

If repetition is an art
the clouds have lost it -
they fray all ways
against their fathers -
their mothers - in the wind
the family nose goes blunt -

if repetition is an art
the clouds are failures
some bloat up, some break
or fall apart   when they touch
they forget where they are -
their mouths can't say   one thing   not once

if repetition is an art -
the clouds are hopeless
and disappear without a   word
for anything -   who'd be
so mutable as this   each day
if repetition is an art –

9

The cartwheel

In the middle sheen of beach
three girls the giant mirage of the sea
doing cartwheels, backlights two of them with the timing
shape, voice wheeling an X the third just can't,
across and across, her letter
slumps each time:

then   X   she turns *Did you see?*
one perfect somersault, she calls *Did you see that?*
a gull through the wind but the others her friends   on the sand
had looked away she slurs and lumps
can't repeat the shape she drew
that no one saw. Or just the sea.

Hush

There's the silence of space and the silence
of noise-cancelled headphones, the unpunctured
silence of the lake at dusk, that strains   tense in every filament, that waits
for utter flatness. Then there is silence   tied to the baton, the orchestra
like brittle leaves in the big hall,   in hibernation but alive, a roost   -silence of bats, a kind of deafness
that shimmers with potential sound   that shifts upon itself, that strives after
the pure shapes in mind, the quantum   paths that shuffle leather wings across
the universe, the absolute of three
degrees, the examination silence
of the sucked pencil.

Mirror Neurons

What does the hand find, cut off in the dark?
Is anybody not surprised by skin?
How can a way be found over a map that changes
every journey? Skin is not a wall, not fluid,
can the hand not find itself in this mirror,
the true hand, the hand that presses to meet
itself from the depths, through very great depths?

Cut off in the dark over a map that changes
itself from the depths, that presses to meet
itself in this mirror: can the hand not find
the true hand, the hand surprised through skin?
Is any body not every journey? Skin is
at very great depths, not a wall, not fluid.
How can a way be found? What does the hand find?

At the skin every journey is surprised. The skin:
what does the hand find over a map that changes
in this mirror? Is any body not
the true hand, the hand cut off in the dark?
Can the hand not find itself from the depths,
not a wall not fluid, that presses to meet
itself through very great depths. How can a way be found?

Over a map that changes can the hand not find
every journey. Skin is itself in this mirror.
What does the hand find? Not fluid, not a wall
that presses to meet the true hand, the hand
itself from the depths, surprised at skin.
How can a way be found through very great depths.
Is any body not cut off in the dark?

(Oyster)/Contactless

As I press on (locked in Boss
and Rolex, plain pearl links) to the tube
(laptop, FT, jangled change) he's laid   sideways for it (homeless? Streetsleeping?)
    casually (beard, dog-on-a-rope,   all this paraphernalia, the
    plastic carrier bags) - what is the   bracket for this life? what statistic   what (income, terror) makes the rope that
                                           binds him to the niceties of   bows, right from his (pallid) midriff
                                           begging, ties him to the (empty Starbucks) cup   to the dog (mongrel, scallop-eared)
                                                                                             that props him up and holds him (down)
                                                                                             against the (clip-clop) tides of people
                                                                                             as I tap through the gates (clam shut).

13

In arcade ego

In between the penny paddles,
the bikes that kids can race   and crash and race again
round lurid Californian tracks,   cheered on by 3-D porno-girls,   the owner watches on CCTV
the virtual super-cars they drive   the video shoot-em-ups   his breeze-block face scowls   into that inverse dark
                                        starbursting with zombie blood   at the only honest game in town -   a parabolic open throat -
                                                                            small change that spirals down   in aid of what? Remember?
                                                                                                                 Spastics? The lifeboat?

14

The Man with X-ray Eyes

All it takes is practice
to see it route-mapped
in full colour:
the blue network of veins
the red branching trees
cross and cross over

yellow is nerves
knitted and tough
a nylon shopping bag,
connective tissue
mother-of pearl
that winks, submerged

close-up the letters
floating through focus
a toad-spawn
acid information
script
rescript

transcript
calligraphy
the word
that explodes
in the carriage.

Help

Help ! you cry from heated sleep,
Help! far-pitched, anxious, like you've
lost one of the kids again you've no idea which way to turn you've
called down all the tunnels left & right twisted the duvet to a map, entrails
  of the throbbing station that gulps all tiled like swimming baths
    & clatters & squeaks with unseen shoes the platforms & corridors change height
      all the same & never the same twice where we have to catch some last train
        out make some connection where
          you never find how to get home but only wake

Summer

So the clouds decide
and agreement spreads - down by the river
people walk differently - the bridge cups its shadow like a lover
at noon precisely and buses keep on going over and over
while the sky turns in the water
the little fish
upstream
all point to where
things come from.

17

Court of the rocking-horse

The legs were broken and badly repaired
with fibreglass – for patching cars – a big
gouge out of the back too, made worse by
an attempted cover-up. It had fallen
we told the restorer. He looked at it,

the Polyfilla, like evidence of torture
in the garage, a terrible accident,
frowned like a surgeon called too late,
he was a local man, obsessive,
        hard as making one new,

but able to operate, just, he said:
it took him two months 'pretty solid',
expensive, but a beautiful job, we all saw,
the shine of grey dapple, the real hair of the tail,
        clean, without fault,   eagle-eyed.

Porlock permeable block

The bloke next door is having new
block paving laid, shearing the scarred
tarmac with a hoarse yellow machine. The work
dusty, muscled but unskilled
- my neighbour - ex-rugby lock - comes out once a while to check the job,
and reckon like an expert in straight lines,
the way he sits in judgement on his pint:

employs two lads (cash-in-hand I bet)
in syncopated chink and scrape: he
he'll tell me all about the deal he struck
let drop how many K he can afford,
I can hear the happy 'plink' when
each brick elbows in.

Low cost repairs

It is worn and dirty and bad
for the tyres, but we can't afford

Tarmac or blocks, so another   load of gravel, that chippy
extemporisation, the short-run   low-cost option on a future
re-drowned to a level flood   symmetric, democratically
                                      eclectic and shifty over
                                      time. How long we hold on for

fractal handfuls, flattering
history, that kind of smooth
recovery: the minister rattles out
layer on layer of slogans and
click-clack, the questions efface.

Moth hunters

Smell the darkness –
cut grass, flowers in musk, the hot
sweet, slow-mo breath of hedgerow –
vegetable truth all round,
    moist excarnation,
where tender lobworms nose & suckle,
fatten on the spittle of the earth.   the crotch of night throws off the bedclothes
    watched by the voyeur's moon, that longs to
    be worm-like - touch and slide, spread on the pubic grass,   night stocks
    persuade the flesh to loosen and be drunk,   receive the delicate proboscis of the moth
    like flower-souls, adapt our drowsy words -   into that sweetness, the soft ruck
        that it inseminates precisely – the mouth
        grown only for this moth, that softens
        and returns the faith in adaptation.

Of thonganomics

Once I could walk the whole half-floor
of menswear and see only signs to 'slacks'
or 'blouses', underwear was, well, under:
a few years back came the 'intimate' range
then 'flirty' sized for the largest

behind. Look at it now
out in the open on the main aisle
of ladies – posters past life scale, near
naked – so the crisis of capital
excess, infinite cheapness, starts here

wall-to-wall, pink, black, mesh, almost
pointless variety, product on product
and we wear ourselves out in the foreplay
of choices, brighter, thinner,
        all the way from India
        all the way from Bangladesh.

By consent

They still look as though they're in
'The Ladybird Book of Policemen'   with their odd pointy hats,
a fifties black-and-white parade -   time warps – you are one side   in the heat-jelly neon dark,
collectively the 'now then' 'evenin all'   turned brute actor when the profile fits -   means trouble - no chance now for
falling round a stage chasing pirates   it's no laughing matter on nights when   singing is aggression, but surrender -
          to go out like this - bared skin   makes the smell that brings in black
          -and-whites, spreading blue contusions.

The view back

Ultraviolet above the drop: heather,
clouds that shove their clumsy-graceful
thumbs in the hill. Rock & the wind,   tight dialogues of erosion
the talking voice of stunted trees   & the angled scratch of shadows,
that pull in very close to the tiny   scrawled tracks, a cuneiform   in the mud, like a photograph
of texture, half-legible, the print   of a forgotten face, a face
like the flash and stink of flint   that jerks the gut like any drop:
struck flint, stunned light
a choice of ways: ultraviolet.

The Prize

Over and over you join in:
raise the left hand, palm flat
faced across the ribcage,   now mirror with the right,
two corrugated wads of flesh,   this is your start, so poised,
suspended, caging in the guts,   jerk them together, crack the air,   let loose and feel these hands
                                     join in and share in slap and sting,   make hymns that manufacture right,
                                     hear and breathe one thing,   do this to empty out the lungs,
                                                                               to roughen up the blood and air,
                                                                               join in to prove it's over.

Talking pictures

Jealous? You bet. Look at the ease
the brush has, across the canvas
left-right, that big purple see-saw
with yellow, would take him what
I spend to cut one word: look

where the trees descend, the green water
fifteen minutes work? That's how long
it takes   one picture to make 50 grand -

the compressed riches
as this blue accelerates it

where everything's on show at once
bulked in space, and that canvas gap
straight at you, untouched by brush,
the virgin world re-told by doing
nothing.

A drill for trust

We fall back how we fall
we fall arms   white after white
backs fall   hung on the tall glass plate   over and over
in nightfall   as wings as trees as grass   we fall back or half fall
through the dark wall   backs hinged   from the ball of the heel
calves falling   each loose crucifix   dropped on the cold waterfall
like a handkerchief   night over night   we sprawl
we spread   half first   we fall back
half last   how we fall
we fall arms
backs fall

The falling

Down falls a lime-key, past the car
one mote on the palest of blue grey,
a pigeon sky that perhaps means snow
the leaf thrums, wobbles and twists,
scribes a wide spiral, dances

for the tarnished November gardens
the nimble parachute talks of air
down, out of control but always
hung lightly between weathers
cars and houses, monomaniac

always down at the windscreen
the lustres of privet and fossil
trees: the small cold nut tracks
down the made, obeyed music
of flight from or to, towards

Acknowledgements

Summer' first appeared in a book of photographs and poems called *Bedford and the River great Ouse* in 2015 (self-published by Darren Marsh, the photographer).

Lightning Source UK Ltd.
Milton Keynes UK
UKHW031934190321
380664UK00001B/16